SCRIPTURE NOVENAS

Novena to Overcome Fear

BOOKS & MEDIA
Boston

Texts of the New Testament used in this work are taken from *The New Testament, St. Paul Catholic Edition,* translated by Mark A. Wauck, copyright © 2000, Daughters of St. Paul. All rights reserved.

Texts of the Psalms used in this work are translated by Manuel Miguens, copyright © Daughters of St. Paul.

All other Old Testament scripture quotations are from the *New Revised Standard Version Bible, Catholic Edition,* copyright © 1993 and 1989 by the Division of Christian Education of the National Council of the Churches of Christ in the U.S.A. Used by permission. All rights reserved.

ISBN 0-8198-5151-5

Copyright © 2000, Daughters of St. Paul

Printed and published in the U.S.A. by Pauline Books & Media, 50 Saint Pauls Avenue, Boston MA 02130-3491.

www.pauline.org

Pauline Books & Media is the publishing house of the Daughters of St. Paul, an international congregation of women religious serving the Church with the communications media.

1 2 3 4 5 6 7   05 04 03 02 01 00

BOOKS & MEDIA

The Daughters of St. Paul operate book and media centers at the following addresses. Visit, call or write the one nearest you today, or find us on the World Wide Web, www.pauline.org

CALIFORNIA
3908 Sepulveda Blvd., Culver City, CA 90230; 310-397-8676
5945 Balboa Ave., San Diego, CA 92111; 858-565-9181
46 Geary Street, San Francisco, CA 94108; 415-781-5180

FLORIDA
145 S.W. 107th Ave., Miami, FL 33174; 305-559-6715

HAWAII
1143 Bishop Street, Honolulu, HI 96813; 808-521-2731
Neighbor Islands call: 800-259-8463

ILLINOIS
172 North Michigan Ave., Chicago, IL 60601; 312-346-4228

LOUISIANA
4403 Veterans Memorial Blvd., Metairie, LA 70006; 504-887-7631

MASSACHUSETTS
Rte. 1, 885 Providence Hwy., Dedham, MA 02026; 781-326-5385

MISSOURI
9804 Watson Rd., St. Louis, MO 63126; 314-965-3512

NEW JERSEY
561 U.S. Route 1, Wick Plaza, Edison, NJ 08817; 732-572-1200

NEW YORK
150 East 52nd Street, New York, NY 10022; 212-754-1110
78 Fort Place, Staten Island, NY 10301; 718-447-5071

OHIO
2105 Ontario Street (at Prospect Ave.), Cleveland, OH 44115; 216-621-9427

PENNSYLVANIA
9171-A Roosevelt Blvd., Philadelphia, PA 19114; 215-676-9494

SOUTH CAROLINA
243 King Street, Charleston, SC 29401; 843-577-0175

TENNESSEE
4811 Poplar Ave., Memphis, TN 38117; 901-761-2987

TEXAS
114 Main Plaza, San Antonio, TX 78205; 210-224-8101

VIRGINIA
1025 King Street, Alexandria, VA 22314; 703-549-3806

CANADA
3022 Dufferin Street, Toronto, Ontario, Canada M6B 3T5; 416-781-9131
1155 Yonge Street, Toronto, Ontario, Canada M4T 1W2; 416-934-3440

¡También somos su fuente para libros, videos y música en español!

To recall throughout the day

***With the Lord as my light
    and my salvation, who can I fear?
With the Lord as my life's stronghold,
    of whom can I be afraid?***

Psalm 27:1

Closing prayer (page 12)

Jesus Calms Our Fears

Opening prayer (page 11)

For meditation

"Let not your hearts be troubled!
Believe in God and believe in me.
In my Father's house are many rooms;
were it not so, would I have told you that I'm
   going to prepare a place for you?
And if I go and prepare a place for you,
I'll come again and take you to myself,
so that where I am,
you, too, may be."

John 14:1–3

To recall throughout the day

***With the Lord as my light
    and my salvation, who can I fear?
With the Lord as my life's stronghold,
    of whom can I be afraid?***

Psalm 27:1

Closing prayer (*page 12*)

YAHWEH, WE TRUST IN YOU!

Opening prayer *(page 11)*

For meditation

I overhear a whispering campaign;
terror comes from every side.
When they, as one, took counsel against me,
they plotted to take my life.
I, instead, trusted in you, O LORD.

I said: "You are my God.
My life's fortunes are in your hands;
deliver me from the hands of my enemies
   and from my persecutors.
Let your face beam on your servant;
save me in your loving kindness."

Psalm 31:14–17

To recall throughout the day

**With the Lord as my light
 and my salvation, who can I fear?
With the Lord as my life's stronghold,
 of whom can I be afraid?**

Psalm 27:1

Closing prayer (page 12)

IN CONFIDENCE, WE PLACE OUR HOPE IN CHRIST

Opening prayer (page 11)

For meditation

"Are not sparrows sold for a few cents? Yet not one of them will fall to the earth without your Father's leave. But as for you, even the hairs of your head are all numbered. So do not be afraid; you are worth more than many sparrows.

"Therefore, whoever acknowledges me before men,
I, too, will acknowledge them before my Father in Heaven."

Matthew 10:29–32

or, 'What will we put on?' for the Gentiles seek all those things. Your Heavenly Father knows you need them! But first seek the Kingdom and the will of God and all those things will be given to you also."

Matthew 6:25–26, 31–33

To recall throughout the day

> **With the Lord as my light**
> **and my salvation, who can I fear?**
> **With the Lord as my life's stronghold,**
> **of whom can I be afraid?**

Psalm 27:1

Closing prayer (*page 12*)

God Cares Deeply for Us

Opening prayer (page 11)

For meditation

"Therefore, I tell you,
don't worry about your life,
   what you'll eat,
or about your body,
   what you'll wear;
is not life more than food,
and the body more than clothing?

   "Look at the birds of the sky—they neither sow nor reap nor gather into barns, yet your Heavenly Father feeds them; are you not worth more than they are? So do not go worrying, saying, 'What will we eat?' or, 'What will we drink?'

will hand him a scorpion?
So if you who are evil know how
   to give good gifts to your children,
all the more will the Father from Heaven
   give the Holy Spirit to those who ask him."

Luke 11:9–13

To recall throughout the day

**With the Lord as my light
   and my salvation, who can I fear?
With the Lord as my life's stronghold,
   of whom can I be afraid?**

Psalm 27:1

Closing prayer (page 12)

God Always Hears Us

Opening prayer (page 11)

For meditation

"And to you I say,
Ask! And it shall be given to you;
Seek! And you shall find;
Knock! And it shall be opened to you.
For everyone who asks, receives;
And whoever seeks will find;
And to those who knock it shall
   be opened.
But is there a father among you who,
   if his son asks for a fish,
instead of a fish will hand him a snake?
Or if he asks for an egg,

21

In its silent trust,
my soul looks to God alone.
It is from him that my salvation can come.
He alone is my rock-solid stronghold and
 my salvation—my bastion.
I cannot waver at all.

Psalm 62:2–3

To recall throughout the day

**With the Lord as my light
 and my salvation, who can I fear?
With the Lord as my life's stronghold,
 of whom can I be afraid?**

Psalm 27:1

Closing prayer (page 12)

GOD REMEMBERS US ALWAYS

Opening prayer *(page 11)*

For meditation

But Zion said,
"The LORD has forsaken me,
my Lord has forgotten me."
Can a woman forget her nursing child,
and show no compassion for the child
  of her womb?
Even these may forget,
yet I will not forget you.
See, I have inscribed you on the palms
  of my hands…

Isaiah 49:14–16

even then would I keep trusting.
One thing have I asked of the Lord,
at this will I take aim:
that I may dwell in the house of the Lord
    all the days of my life,
gazing on the goodness of the Lord
    and seeking guidance in his Temple.
For he will conceal me in his pavilion
    on an evil day
        and hide me in the shelter of his tent;
he will set me high on a rock.

Psalm 27:1–5

To recall throughout the day

With the Lord as my light
    and my salvation, who can I fear?
With the Lord as my life's stronghold,
    of whom can I be afraid?

Psalm 27:1

Closing prayer *(page 12)*

OF WHOM SHOULD WE BE AFRAID?

Opening prayer (page 11)

For meditation

With the Lord as my light and my salvation,
   who can I fear?
With the Lord as my life's stronghold,
   of whom can I be afraid?
When evildoers drew near to me
   to devour my flesh,
when my adversaries and enemies
   were against me,
      it was they who stumbled and fell.
Should an army encamp against me,
   my heart would not fear;
should war rage against me,

To recall throughout the day

*With the Lord as my light
  and my salvation, who can I fear?
With the Lord as my life's stronghold,
  of whom can I be afraid?*

Psalm 27:1

Closing prayer (page 12)

We Do Not Fear Because We Belong to Yahweh

Opening prayer (page 11)

For meditation

Thus says the LORD who made you,
   who formed you in the womb,
      and will help you:
Do not fear, O Jacob my servant,
   Jeshurun whom I have chosen.
For I will pour water on the thirsty land,
   and streams on the dry ground;
I will pour my spirit upon your descendants,
   and my blessing on your offspring.
They shall spring up like green tamarisk,
   like willow trees by flowing streams.

Isaiah 44:2–4

Abandon yourself to the Lord and
   wait for him.
The salvation of the righteous comes
   from the Lord,
their stronghold in times of distress.
So the Lord will help and deliver them;
he will deliver and save them from the wicked
for they have taken refuge in him.

Psalm 37:7, 39–40

To recall throughout the day

With the Lord as my light
   and my salvation, who can I fear?
With the Lord as my life's stronghold,
   of whom can I be afraid?

Psalm 27:1

Closing prayer *(page 12)*

WITH GOD WE HAVE NOTHING TO FEAR

Opening prayer *(page 11)*

For meditation

But in all these things we are winning an overwhelming victory through the One who loved us. I'm convinced that neither death nor life, neither angels nor principalities, neither things present nor to come nor powers, neither height nor depth nor any other created being will be able to separate us from God's love in Christ Jesus our Lord.

Romans 8:37–39

Closing Prayer
(for each day)

O God, in confidence we have come before you, trusting that you desire our well-being even more than we ourselves desire it. Fill our hearts with your Spirit, so that when we are faced with the difficulties and anxieties that life brings, we may remember your eternal love, and trust in the promise of your presence. Through your Son, Jesus Christ our Lord, in the unity of the Holy Spirit, one God forever and ever. Amen.

Opening Prayer
(for each day)

O God, you are the source of freedom from all fear and anguish. Look with kindness on our weaknesses. Although we are certain of your love for us, anxiety and worry often assail us. But you are with us as our Father. You defend us, protect us, and love us. Help us not to be afraid! Through your Son, our Lord Jesus Christ, in the unity of the Holy Spirit, one God forever and ever. Amen.

barren and dry, anxious and afraid. Try to open your heart to hear the Lord speaking to you about your situation. Pay attention to any unexpected thoughts or feelings that arise during your prayer…is God extending any invitations to you regarding your prayer intentions?

As you come to the end of your prayer time, spend some moments silently recalling the day's theme. End your prayer time by praying an ***Our Father, Hail Mary, Glory Be,*** and the ***Closing Prayer.***

To be done on a daily basis

For nine consecutive days, set apart time for quiet reflection on the true meaning of your life. The title given to each day is the theme for that day. Try to center your meditation on the biblical thoughts suggested for the day in light of this theme, and bear in mind your own needs and desires.

Remind yourself that you are in God's presence. Ask God to bless you and all those you love as you hold in your heart the persons and intentions that you especially desire to pray for. Confidently express these intentions to God.

Pray the **Opening Prayer,** and then begin to meditate on the day's scripture passage. Allow a slow, peaceful repetition of the Word of God to nourish whatever within you may be aside, because fear has to do with punishment, and a person who is afraid is not perfected in love" (1 John 4:18). Perhaps concentrating on *loving* rather than *fearing* is the first step toward inner freedom.

As we pray with God's word, we hear the Lord inviting us to a deeper experience of God's love and care for us.

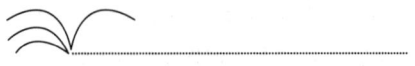

NOVENA TO OVERCOME FEAR

Fear comes in many sizes. It can be as small as occasional butterflies in the stomach, or as crippling as recurring panic attacks which prevent normal daily living. Fear can sometimes be helpful, such as the fear of being hit by a car, which makes us pause before crossing the street. Yet, most of the time, fear is unproductive. Jesus said so himself: "Fear is useless; what is needed is trust" (Mark 5:36).

In the Gospel, Jesus repeatedly tells us not to be afraid because he is with us and will not abandon us. He has even given us a secret for overcoming fear; it involves increasing the quality of our love. "Perfect love casts all fear

may appear to be mere repetition in a novena is really a continual act of faith and hope in our loving God.

Like the rosary, the Stations of the Cross, the Liturgy of the Hours, or meal prayers, novenas are one small part of our Catholic faith. The greatest prayer of all is the Eucharistic Celebration. The Eucharist is central to Catholic living; from this great source flows the answer to all our human longings. Through praying with Scripture in this novena, may we draw near our Eucharistic God with confidence, "to receive mercy and find grace to help us in time of need" (Hebrews 4:16).

always prayed for various needs, trusting that God both hears and answers prayer. Over time, the custom of praying for nine consecutive days for a particular need came to be called praying "a novena," since *novena* means *nine*.

There are many different kinds of novenas, but their purpose is the same: we call to mind our needs and we ask God's help and protection while remembering how much God loves us. And as we pray, we also ask for a greater understanding and acceptance of God's mysterious workings in our life and the lives of those we love.

"But," we might wonder, "doesn't God know our needs before we even ask; isn't praying once for something enough?" Although we believe in God's love for us, sometimes we need to remind ourselves of this. Although we know we are held in God's hands and that God will not let go, sometimes we need reassurance. In times of darkness, we need something to hold on to; in times of joy, we want to keep rejoicing! What

What Is a Novena?

Most families have traditions—cherished customs and practices handed on from one generation to another. A novena is like that—a Catholic "family tradition," a type of prayer that is one of the ways our family of faith has prayed for centuries.

The Catholic tradition of praying novenas comes from the earliest days of the Church. After the ascension of Jesus, the Acts of the Apostles tells us that the Apostles and Mary gathered together and "devoted themselves single-mindedly to prayer" (Acts 1:14). And on the day of Pentecost, the Spirit of the Lord came to them. Based on this, Christians have